THE KOREAN REVIVAL

THE KOREAN REVIVAL

by

RENÉ MONOD

Translated by
ANTHEA BELL

With a foreword by
DR. BILLY GRAHAM

HODDER AND STOUGHTON
LONDON   SYDNEY   AUCKLAND   TORONTO

FOREWORD

The Korean Church has set a pattern of perennial revival to which the Church universal looks with wonder and amazement. When I visited Korea years ago I was astounded to find Christians getting up two hours before daylight, and gathering in their churches for prayer, Bible reading and testimony. The scenes I witnessed there have stayed with me through the years, and have had a great impact on my personal, spiritual life.

It is refreshing to know that the spirit of revival still prevails in Korea, and that the work of God there continues unabated. At the alarming rate of spiritual decline in the West, it is conceivable that God is getting Koreans ready to serve as missionaries to the Western Church. For years the flow of missionaries was from west to east, but it is possible that in the Providence of God that may be reversed in the future. In any event, the Korean Church stands as a beacon of spiritual light in an area of darkness.

In this book on the Korean Revival René Monod gives us some of the fascinating stories of changed lives, and transformed communities in that battle-scarred land. It is the saga of a people who have suffered, who have been persecuted, but have emerged as spiritual giants in an environment which only divine grace could make so productive.

BILLY GRAHAM

CONTENTS

IN SEARCH OF SPIRITUAL LIFE

Many Christian communities of the Western world today resemble graveyards. The church tower is a gigantic gravestone, bearing witness to the fact that devout men and women once built themselves a place of worship here. The sound of bells no longer serves to call those in the world around to the house of God; it is generally considered a mere source of noise, and protests from the inhabitants of large cities have sometimes led to a state of affairs where bell-ringing is confined to a minimum. When the pastor stands at the altar he sees rows of empty pews before him. I can myself testify to the fact that of the 60,000 'members of the congregation' of a certain cathedral city in Western Europe, only 200 attended divine service; seen another way, this means that only one in every 300 nominal Christians of this community deigned to pay his respects to the Lord on a Sunday.

However, this brief account of matters should not be regarded as a sweeping judgment. Even in the Western hemisphere, congregations of devout and faithful Christians are still to be found. I could give many examples, such as the communities of the Brazilian Established Church in Blumenau and Rio de Janeiro. Or I might point to Dr. McGee's congregation in Los Angeles. He has 4000 worshippers at Sunday service, and 2000 people attend his weekly Bible class. We need not search in vain on European soil either. Spiritual life flourishes in the evangelical congregation of Samuel Vila in Spain, and

Pastor Blocher's Tabernacle in Paris. I could mention Pastor Meyer-Schomburg's evangelical congregation in Vienna, or the Westminster Chapel in London. What of Germany? Despite the current secularisation of life in that country, there are oases of spiritual life in Germany too; it would be only right to mention the many Swabian villages who have not yet welcomed modern theology, 'the darling child of Hell', into their midst.

In spite of these staunch outposts of spiritual life in the Western hemisphere, however, we may look around us in vain for a Christian revival. The last great revival of the West took place in Wales in 1905. The spiritual awakening in the Scottish Hebrides in 1949 was confined to a few islands, and had no effect on the country as a whole.

The four great revivals of recent decades have been gifts given to non-European countries, occurring in Korea (1906 onwards), Uganda (1927), Formosa (1945), and Indonesia (1965). This account of the religious awakening of Korea sets out to give it life and meaning for Western readers.

Chapter I

THE REVIVAL IN KOREA

1. The Political History of Korea

The historical background of Korean history can be quickly sketched. The Korean peninsula, an area almost as large as that of the Federal Republic of Germany, lies between the Yellow Sea and the Sea of Japan. Korea was a bone of contention between China and Japan for 2000 years, coming under Russian protection and influence for a brief eight-year period, from 1897 to 1905, when the ruling Yi dynasty, becoming increasingly weak, could no longer deal with the country's political and economic problems. In 1905 the Russo-Japanese war broke out, and after the war the Japanese had the upper hand in Korea. In 1920, Korea was officially annexed by Japan, and Japanese supremacy in the country lasted until the end of the Second World War. The Allies then divided Korea into zones; the Russians moved into the north zone, the Americans into the south zone, and the border was formed by the 38th Parallel.

There was discord between North and South Korea. Negotiations to have elections held throughout the whole country broke down. In 1948, South Korea was proclaimed a republic, by the name of Taihan, and Syngman Rhee became its first president. Then, in June 1950, the accursed attempt of the Communists to seize political power began. They crossed the demarcation line; the advance was made mainly by Red Chinese troops. After the vicissitudes of the war, the Communists were pushed back, and the 38th Parallel again became the border, with some small amendments.

The wave of persecution of North Korean Christians brought a great influx of refugees south. Subsequently, as a precaution against possible further Communist attacks, the Americans provided South Korea with economic and military aid.

The South Koreans consider their allies timid. The Americans lost prestige in South Korea when they allowed the *Pueblo* to be seized, and a plane shot down by North Korea, without making reprisals.

It is against the backdrop of these political developments that we see the spiritual events concerning Christianity in Korea played out.

2. *The Spiritual Development of Korea*

I learned the story of the revival during my two visits to Korea. My principal source of information is Dr. Blair, who, at the time I write this, is ninety-two years old, and living in a Presbyterian old people's home in Los Angeles. He is the last surviving first-hand witness of the revival.

My second source consists of the verbal and written accounts given me by Dr. Han, a prominent and well-known minister in Korea, who is a close friend of Dr. Blair. Dr. Han lived and worked with Dr. Blair for years. He is, however, not a direct witness, since he was only a small boy at the start of the revival.

My third witness is Dr. Lee. He did missionary work in Korea, and conducted many revivalist meetings. Dr. Lee is no longer alive, but when I was in Seoul I heard his account of the revival.

Before describing the revival itself, I must first outline the rise of the Christian mission in Korea.

The first emissary to bring the Gospel to Korea was the medical missionary Dr. C. Allen, who set foot on Korean soil in 1845. He was sent out by the Presbyterian Church of the United States of America.

Another landmark in the early story of the Christian mission was an event with an unhappy outcome. This was the missionary venture of the Welshman, Robert Thomas. He had been working in China as a representative of the Scottish Bible Society, and on hearing that educated people in Korea could read Chinese, he conceived the idea of taking Bibles there.

In 1866 Brother Thomas found an American schooner, the *General Sherman*, sailing for Pyengyang in North Korea. As the ship approached the coast, the half-savage Korean coastguards showed hostility, throwing burning brands on deck. The fire and smoke drove the crew into the sea. A number saved themselves in one of the ship's boats, but they were captured and killed by the coast-guards. Taking his stock of Bibles with him, Brother Thomas waded through the shallow water to land, where he was met with blows. However, he was able to press his Bibles into the hands of his murderers before he collapsed and died. And so the soil of North Korea drank the blood of a martyr on the very same spot where, forty years later, the revival took place. In this way the sacrifice of the life of one of the early missionaries sowed the seed of the Korean Church.

The isolation of Korea, and its primitive way of life, could hardly last for ever. In 1876 the Japanese forced an entry into several ports; they were to be opened to other naval powers some years later. Korea officially opened her gates to the world in 1884.

Presbyterian and Methodist missions saw this as their chance. The missionaries Horace Underwood and Henry Appenzeller, with their wives, came to Korea. Their work spread rapidly. Around the turn of the century mission stations could be found in all the larger towns. A theological seminary was founded, and in 1907 it was turning out the first trained ministers for field work. At the same time the Presbyterian Church of Korea was set up, and began its work. From the start, these missionary ventures were under pro-American auspices.

The situation soon altered when America sanctioned the Japanese occupation of Korea. Korean Christians were torn between their allegiance to Christianity and their allegiance to their country. In this state of mental conflict, they threw themselves entirely on the mercy of God. They were not to regret it.

The missionaries were unfortunately placed in this tense political situation. In a state of national and social chaos, they had no recourse but to prayer. Having exhausted their own resources of wisdom, they prayed for the guidance of the Holy Spirit. They began to hold prayer meetings, and continued for over a year. In the winter of 1906, a Bible class met in the central Presbyterian church in Pyengyang; it recruited many Christians from the other towns and districts. The attendance grew until there were some 1000 or 1200 people present. An impulse towards purification began to be felt at the prayer meetings. Confession of sins, acknowledgment of the holiness of God, the casting out of the old Adam — these were the biblical truths that were staring them in the face. In addition, they felt an increasing desire for an enduringly prayerful way of life, and the sanctification of the daily round.

As these prayer meetings went on, there came a certain Monday when the missionaries felt quite clearly that God was close to them. A service was arranged for that evening, in Pyengyang (now written Pyongyang), and the whole assembled congregation was taken into the presence of the Lord. After a short sermon, Dr. Lee called upon them to pray. Many began to pray out loud at the same time. Hitherto the missionaries had not permitted this mode of prayer, abiding by the rule laid down in the Bible (I Corinthians 14: 27): 'Let it be by two, or at the most by three, and that by course.' At this service, however, the missionaries could feel an almost overpowering tension in the air, a great urge to pray, and Dr. Lee said, 'If it helps you all to pray together, then pray in that way.'

Then a tide began to sweep through the church. There was no confusion; it was a single harmony of prayer, as if the voices of all the praying congregation merged together to form a single cry to God. There was not the slightest disorder. The Holy Ghost welded them all together into one. As on the day of the first Whitsun, all souls were tuned to the same note, and unity of the spirit held sway.

I must here make a comment in passing. Simultaneous prayer by all those present at a meeting is practised in many parts of the world. The Quaker missionaries in Alaska make use of it, as do the Keswickites in Japan, in Australia and other countries. Communal prayer is practised in several mission groups in Africa, for instance, in Zuenoula on the Ivory Coast, and in many Pentecostal communities. There is a great difference between communal prayer inspired by the Holy Ghost and communal prayer that merely represents a fading tradition harking back to some great event in the past. In general, traditions and imitations lack the wonderful harmony of the Holy Ghost.

But at the time of the revival in Korea, this mode of simultaneous prayer partook of the original inspiration of the Holy Ghost.

3. The Effects of the Revival

At this great prayer meeting one worshipper after another rose, confessed his sins, and then fell to his knees again, weeping and begging God for forgiveness. Employees confessed their sins to their employers and vice versa. Elders of the Church asked their ministers for forgiveness. The ministers made their peace with one another, repenting of their petty jealousies. All sins were confessed, not only sins of commission, but the sins of the tongue and the mind as well.

It is indeed wonderful to think how the Holy Ghost works in the same way in revivals all over the world. Exactly the same thing happened during the Ugandan revival, twenty years later than the revival in Korea. We find the same biblical phenomena in the Indonesian revival of the present day. At a certain Javanese institute prayer would continue for half the night; the Spirit of God brought about the acknowledgment of sins in teachers as well as pupils. They asked one another for forgiveness, and the whole atmosphere was cleansed.

The Spirit of God often — nay, always! — has the same design. He shows us our sins, He shows us our redemption. He breaks down our stubborn hearts, purifies the relationships of men with one another, and builds the Church of Jesus. It was so in Jerusalem after the first descent of the Holy Ghost, and it has been so in all genuine revivals.

In Korea, the people were so carried away by their urge to repent and confess their sins that each forgot his own self, and stood only in the presence of God. Even the old missionaries did not escape the tide of repentance and purification sweeping through the congregation. All human authority and power became as nothing before the face of God. Many of those present simply lay prostrate on the floor, oppressed and cast down by the weight of their own sins.

The missionaries were no longer in command of the situation. Finally, they assembled on the platform and asked each other, 'What are we to do? If this goes on, some of them will go out of their minds.' But they dared not interrupt. They had been praying for the Holy Ghost to come down for weeks, and now God had granted their prayer. They felt they had no right to put out this flame.

At last they agreed to walk among the ranks of the people, comforting those who were most overwhelmed. They raised many from the ground, consoling them with a text from the Bible promising forgiveness. Then Dr. Lee struck up a hymn, and after they had sung it they continued praying as before.

It was impossible to bring the meeting to a close forcibly. The Korean congregation had lost all need to eat and sleep, only one thing still seemed important to their souls — to make their peace with God.

In normal times one may discuss whether public confession of sins is right or not. Of course every biblically orientated minister with experience in the cure of souls would advise against it, and rightly so. But when the Holy Ghost descends upon a congregation — genuinely descends, and the visitation is genuine when it is caused by the Spirit of God and not the human spirit — then other rules come into force. It would have been unwise of the missionaries in Korea to try to stop this movement of confession and repentance. In so doing, they would have been restraining the power of the Holy Ghost, no less. Moreover, it would have been impossible to tell these penitents of North Korea to stop confessing their sins aloud; the Spirit of God was in command, and no earthly wisdom. It would be beside the mark, however, for a psychologist to say, 'Koreans are naturally more emotional and unstable in the way they express their feelings than Europeans'. There is no truth in such an idea; Korea is as cold a country as Germany, spring comes in Seoul later than in France and England, Pyongyang is in fact appreciably colder than Western Europe, and the Koreans are in no way less stable than the French or the Germans.

When the Holy Ghost breaks in on human souls, psychological aspects need no longer concern us. Of course, a southerner has a warmer temperament than a northerner, but the Holy Ghost can break down a cold man's defences as easily as those of a more hot-blooded man. In considering the acts of the Holy Ghost, we are concerned not with temperamental characteristics, but with the state of a man's heart.

In these days of the revival, there were meetings of penitents in Pyongyang that went on all night. Let us hear a first-hand account from Dr. Blair:

Every sin that a man can commit was publicly confessed that first night. They stood in the blinding light of God's judgment, pale and trembling, in almost mortal conflict between body and soul. They saw themselves as God saw them. Their sins arose before them in all their disgrace and shame. They none of them made excuses for themselves; they simply assented, taking all the blame upon their own shoulders. All pride was cast down. They looked up to Heaven, to Jesus, and acknowledged that they had betrayed him. Weeping bitterly and beating their breasts, they cried, 'Lord, do not cast us out for ever!' Every other consideration was forgotten; nothing else had any meaning. What did the wrath of men mean to them now, or the legal sentences that might eventually threaten them? Death itself seemed to have no more importance to these people, if only God would forgive them their sins. We may think as we will on this matter, but when the Holy Ghost strikes down a man in his guilt, there will be confession of sins, and no power on earth can prevent it.

4. *The Spread of the Movement*

The revival began in Pyongyang, now the Communist capital of North Korea. The students from the theological seminary were present when these great meetings for the purpose of confession and repentance took place; they were all carried away by the spirit of the revival, and then, as young ministers, they carried the flame out into all the land.

Everywhere these young emissaries of Jesus went similar gatherings of penitents met to pray. At times teachers in the schools could not go on with their lessons, because their pupils were confessing their sins and asking for forgiveness. Villages and districts where no missionary had ever worked before were infected with enthusiasm when they heard the reports. Deadly enemies made their peace with one another; stolen money and goods were returned. Past injustices were set right, not only between Christians, but to pagans as well. One old Chinese businessman was much surprised when a Christian returned a large sum of money which he had once received from the merchant in error. Many heathens were converted and brought to Christ by the honourable conduct of these Christians.

The fire kindled by the Holy Ghost burnt on. Those Koreans who had been affected by the revival set themselves the task of spreading the Gospel through the whole of Korea within a year. They raised large sums to carry the message to regions where no missionary had ever been. As an aid to their evangelical work, they had an edition of a million copies of the Gospel according to St. Mark printed, and sold 700,000 in a single year. Even this was not enough; they sent missionaries abroad. One settled in Vladivostock in Siberia, to care for the Koreans living there. Others were sent to remote islands; others again travelled in China. At this time the so-called 'Movement of the Millions', a child of the Korean revival, came into being. The expression is well known from the work of the China Inland Mission, one of whose publications bore the title, 'China's Millions'.

The revival marked the birth of the Christian Church in Korea, a Church that is spiritually still very much alive today, despite all the shadows through which it has passed.

To sum up the main features of the revival: this spiritual awakening in Korea was a penitential and confessional movement. Men and women came flocking to the Lord Jesus. The 'gift of tongues' was not a part of this revival. It is necessary to emphasise this point, since today the question of the 'gift of tongues' causes some confusion in the Church of Jesus. To avoid misunderstanding, I must point out that all the spiritual gifts mentioned in the New Testament are, of course, to be recognised; what we have to do is learn to tell the difference between charismatic and psychic phenomena.

5. *Charismatic Side-effects*

Every revival produces its offshoots, and sometimes even dangerous reactionary movements, a fact often to be attributed to retaliation on the part of the dark powers. The Devil will not stand idly by when the Spirit of God kindles a flame. Indeed, it sometimes happens that a very bright light casts particularly dark shadows.

Almost every revival of the present century has been accompanied by manifestations of healing, a phenomenon familiar to us from the Bible. In many cases, when the relationship of man with God is set right the healing of bodily infirmities will follow too. Moreover, a man freed from all his burdens stands in a different relationship of prayer to God from that of a nominal Christian who is unacquainted with the true life of prayer. The promises of the Bible shine out before the reborn man like bright stars to show him his way.

Visionary experiences also occur in all revivals. I heard Dr. Lee's account of the following vision, which he had at the time of the Korean revival. One day he was in a church, praying; it was three o'clock in the afternoon. Then he saw an angel standing in the chancel, and around the church he saw tongues of fire, as at the first Pentecost. There were heathen Koreans at work outside, near the church, and he saw them in the form of animals, not as men.

This vision need not be considered anything at all unusual. The tongues of fire are the symbol of the Holy Ghost. When true Christians pray in their churches, the arm of God is moved, and it is then that 'ministering spirits' (Hebrews 1: 14) appear. The appearance of men in the form of animals is not unprecedented; we can find similar ideas both in heathenism and in Christianity. Buddhists believe that a man who fails to pass the test will find himself reincarnated as an animal in his next life. In Christian cultures, we find allusions in Dante's *Divine Comedy* to wicked and unregenerate men who appear as animals in the Inferno. Such visionary experiences are known to me from my own ministry.

In the context of a revival, then, perfectly genuine charismatic phenomena do occur, and we must not dismiss them as proceeding from an abnormal or fanatical state of mind. However, these side-effects can lead to error when believers deliberately try to bring about ecstatic experiences such as visions or the gift of tongues. Generally speaking, experiences thus forced into existence serve as the gateway to evil spirits, who are only waiting for such open doors (Ephesians 6: 12). Here again the rule holds good: that which the Holy Ghost gives of His own accord is natural and God-given, that which man, striving for extraordinary experiences, tries to force into being is usually no gift of the Holy Ghost, but the dubious gift of quite another spirit.

The death of all revivals is the fatigue that sets in after some years or decades. It is a sad fact that no revival lasts over a century in its original form. Most are of much shorter duration. How does Korea measure up to this situation?

6. *The Time of Trial*

The Korean Church that arose from the revival found itself under political pressures from the start. From 1905 onwards the Japanese who were occupying the country oppressed the Koreans in every way, pursuing a policy of exploitation in the fullest sense of the word. The entire public finances were in the hands of the occupying power. No Korean could aspire to any high economic or political position. The effects were so far-reaching that after the withdrawal of the Japanese there was no one in Korea who could exchange foreign currency. The American missionaries were in no position to support their economically weak congregations. The people themselves were hardly able to meet their own needs. The Japanese had, in fact, taken the line of regarding Korea as a mere marketing area; only Japanese products could be obtained, and there were no indigenous Korean factories.

From the cultural aspect too everything was given a strong Japanese flavour. Only Japanese was used in official communications, and those who could not speak it had to make use of interpreters. Japanese was also introduced into secondary schools as the official language, which caused great distress among the people.

Religious pressure was a source of great affliction and danger to the young Church. On the national festival day, all Koreans had to show their loyalty to the Japanese by attending a ceremony at the Shinto shrine. This meant that Christians had to struggle with their consciences, asking themselves if it was right for people of their religion to bow down at the Shinto shrine.

The leading ministers made representations to the Japanese authorities, asking to be excused from the ceremony on religious grounds. It was explained to them that the rite was of a political and not a religious character. Many Christians were reassured by this answer, and thereafter attended the ceremony. The principal of the theological seminary also complied, so as not to endanger the college's future existence.

Other Christians, in particular those who thought for themselves, pointed out that the rite was not merely a declaration of political loyalty, since all the prayers said in the course of it were of a Shintoist nature. This was a conflict that caused Christians great distress of mind.

Finally, a devout Korean minister ventured to abstain from attending the Shinto ceremony. The result was that the Japanese had him beaten to death near the Shinto shrine. The true situation was clear enough now. However, many Christians did not have this man's courage to bear witness, and compromised. For this reason the revival movement went backwards rapidly at the time of the Japanese occupation. The introduction of the Shinto ceremony had helped to suppress the efficacy of the powers of the Holy Ghost.

Chapter II

THE SECOND WAVE OF THE REVIVAL

Wesley spoke of the 'second blessing', by which he meant that Christians should not rest content with their conversion; God has more than one blessing in store for us. This saying of Wesley's has often been misunderstood, and even raised to the status of a doctrine in extremist circles. But the Spirit of God works in a sovereign way, and cannot be forced into any pattern. It would be a poor God who had only two blessings to give His children. The life of a true Christian is enriched by thousands of blessings. Yet there are individual Christians, and entire movements, that can point to one particular 'second blessing'. We know as much from Charles H. Finney, the travelling evangelist Jakob Vetter, Major Thomas, and many other men of God.

Similarly, the story of the Hebridean revival shows two waves of blessing, the first around 1949, the second beginning in 1953. Unfortunately this movement got into the troubled waters of fanaticism.

In the Korean revival, two stages stand out quite clearly. The first wave of the revival movement was from 1906–45. When the Japanese had withdrawn, the practice of the Shinto cult, so offensive to Christians, also came to an end, and the faithful subjected themselves to a process of purification. But they were not to be permitted to breathe freely for long. New troubles and yet worse persecutions were looming up on the horizon.

1. *The Political Terror in North Korea*

The North Koreans made use of their short period of freedom, between the withdrawal of the Japanese and the coming of the Russians. At the cost of great sacrifices, both of money and the work of their hands, they erected places where they might pray and hear the word of God. This peaceful and constructive work was destroyed again and again by the Communists.

The situation of the Christians became positively desperate when Red Chinese troops entered the country, and the Communists prepared to take over the whole of Korea.

It is strange to think that the city of Pyongyang had been the source of the revival. Under the Communists, the same city became the centre of a new outbreak of persecution of the Christians. One wonders whether this counter-attack may not have been staged by Hell itself?

The opening shot in the persecutors' attack was the arrest of a leading statesman who was a convinced Christian. This politician disappeared without trace, and no one now believes him to be alive.

But the great suffering that came upon the Christians was turned by God into blessing. So long as divine service was not forbidden, the Christians again gathered daily to pray in their churches, as at the time of the revival. Since their premises were not large enough, they prayed outside the churches too. Naturally, this religious movement did not escape the Communists' notice. They therefore closed one church after another, but they could not dam up the stream of prayer. The prayer meetings grew to even larger proportions than those of 1906–07.

The Christians would meet before sunrise, sometimes around five a.m., often as early as four a.m. No one troubled about the weather; neither cold nor snow nor rain could keep them away. Thousands attended the meetings. They all prayed simultaneously, as in the days when the Holy Ghost had visited Korea.

We can find no other example in ecclesiastical history of 10,000 men and women in prayer directing their pleas to Heaven at a single prayer meeting. Yet even this was not the highest peak. Prominent North Korean Christians claimed that there had been meetings where 12,000 people were together in prayer — and that after thousands of Christians had already fled to South Korea.

Of course there were political informers among those who attended these vast prayer meetings, but what authority wishes to arrest a whole congregation of 12,000 people? However, the Communists picked out the leaders. Yet the spirit of prayer was not to be halted by the Red Terror.

Appalling acts of terrorism by the Communists made many Christians conceive the plan of venturing upon flight to South Korea. Dreadful things happened, as reliable Christian sources have reported. Several Christians were crucified by the Chinese Communists, and hung on their crosses for days until they died in torment. Faithful witnesses who did not cease from spreading the Gospel of Jesus had their tongues cut out by the Red Chinese. Children caught at a secret Sunday School were deafened; inhuman Communists pushed chopsticks into their eardrums and so destroyed their sense of hearing.

These outrages turned the North Korean Church into a catacomb Church, or an underground Church, as we say today. It would be as well for those Western Christians who do not always see clearly to read the books of Pastor Wurmbrand. This author, who was himself tortured by the Communists for fourteen years, has reported many acts of terrorism, and his accounts correspond to the truth, as I was able to confirm myself from the accounts given by Christian refugees.

Those North Korean Christians who saw any chance of making their way to the south embarked upon the dangerous journey, slipping through the front lines. Any who were caught by the Communists died, yet many did succeed in leaving North Korea, its soil now soaked in the blood of martyrs.

2. *Syngman Rhee*

In the years 1945–50, when the Communists were oppressing the people and the land of North Korea, South Korea had two pieces of good fortune.

In the first place, the Christian communities of the south profited by the influx of North Korean refugees. These Christians, tried in the furnace of suffering, brought with them a mighty spirit of prayer, and started up many prayer meetings in the south. We shall hear more of this when we come to look at the Young Nak Church.

The second favourable factor in the life of the Christian community was the figure of South Korea's first President, who was a convinced Christian. Let us hear his story.

Korea is unique in many ways; I know of no other state in the world with a President who could tell how he came to Christ.

At the time of the Japanese occupation, Syngman Rhee was an enthusiastic patriot; his whole endeavour was to see his land and his people freed from the rule of the hated foreigners.

Being in need of money, he was prepared to give language lessons to Christian missionaries, although he disliked the mission, and the missionaries were, to him, only foreigners of whom he would have liked to see his country rid. In the course of the lessons he was giving, however, he realised that these Christian men were well disposed towards his people.

As a resistance fighter, Rhee was on the Japanese black list, which meant that he often had to disappear in order to avoid arrest. On one such occasion he took refuge with an American missionary called Dr. Avison. The Japanese were on his track wherever he went, and so finally he had to go abroad. However, he could not stay away for long; he knew that his life was bound up for better or worse with the fate of Korea. So he returned to Seoul. Shortly afterwards he was arrested and condemned to death.

He was put in the condemned cell, which was only two metres square, and very badly ventilated. To add to this discomfort he was put in the stocks at night — the same instrument of torture as was used on Paul and Silas in prison in Philippi (Acts 16: 24).

Rhee expected to see the executioner every morning. But strange to say, that individual was a long time putting in an appearance. We need not wonder at this, for the hand of God was over the condemned man, although he was not yet a believer. The American missionaries, who had heard of his arrest, prayed fervently for their former teacher.

During this waiting period he asked his warder to borrow a Bible and a dictionary for him from the American missionaries. Again it was the goodness of God that moved the warder to grant this request; in other parts of the world too a condemned man is allowed a last wish.

He read the Bible eagerly. Now, in the loneliness of his cell and near to death, it made a strong appeal to him. And he remembered the words of the missionaries, who had once told him, 'God listens to prayer.'

For the first time in his life, Rhee prayed. 'O God, save

my soul and save my country.' Immediately his cell
seemed to be filled with light, and the peace of God was
with him and refreshed him. From this hour he was a new
man. His hatred of the missionaries and his hatred of the
Japanese had disappeared.

The new convert did the best thing a reborn Christian
can do: he bore witness to his Lord before men. However,
the prison warder was the only person he ever saw. He
therefore told him of his encounter with Jesus, and when
the warder's brother came to the prison to visit him, Rhee
told this man of his experience too. The result of his testimony was that both men were converted. Here again there
is a similarity to the story of St. Paul's prison in Philippi,
where the keeper of the prison was converted.

The condemned man, his warder and the warder's
brother were now all brethren in the spirit, and their
church was the condemned cell. From this time on the
warder acted like that colleague of his in Philippi, who
washed Paul's feet and bound up his wounds. Rhee was
no longer put in the stocks, he got better food, and was
moved to a more comfortable cell.

The great change that had come over their most important prisoner did not escape the notice of the prison's
administrative officers, and when the condemned man
asked permission to open a school for his fellow-prisoners
within the jail, he was allowed to do so. Many of his other
requests were also granted. He could write letters to
people outside, and he received Christian tracts and scrip-
tures from the missionaries. And so a Bible class was
formed in the prison. The time Rhee spent in prison bore
its finest fruit when the warder's brother began to prepare
himself for the ministry. He attended a seminary in America and became a pastor.

It was part of God's plan that Rhee should be set free
again, and as we have already seen, he became the first

President of South Korea. What country on earth can point to an episode of 'political' history like this?

Syngman Rhee preserved his Christian attitude in high office; many of the most important posts in his government were filled by devout Christians. His Chief of General Staff was a faithful churchgoer who never missed a Sunday. Moreover, this General was part-time director of a Christian orphanage. Many pastors became district governors, and the President's personal influence was felt all over the country. He did not become proud in his faith, but remained a humble, devout Christian to his dying day.

3. *The Threat to South Korea*

Syngman Rhee took up his post in 1948. He was not long granted the opportunity to pursue peaceful and constructive ends. In 1950 came the Communist assault from North Korea. The whole country was in a state of great alarm; the people knew from the North Korean refugees what was to be expected, and they viewed the approaching disaster with fear and trembling. The churches were filled. Prayer meetings were held everywhere. One of the strongest of the groups who met to pray was that of the Young Nak Church; it was in this community that most of the North Korean refugees had come together, men and women who had already had to endure what the Red Terror could do once. They were not to know that this second threat was not the end.

The Red Chinese took Seoul, the capital of South Korea, and the members of the government had to go south. Many high-ranking North Koreans also found themselves on the run for the second time. Once again they had lost all they had.

The Communists clung tenaciously to their positions,

until U.N. troops, predominantly American, forced them northward and back behind the demarcation line. During the fighting it was, of all things, American grenades that did most damage to Seoul. A severe blow was the loss of the Bible House, which had been built, with great pains, only a few years earlier, and which now fell victim to the flames. It had just been completely stocked with Bibles and parts of Bibles when the unexpected disaster struck. It seemed as if the suffering would never end. Seoul changed its masters four times before the truce was made. But in spite of all the sufferings of South Korea, the Red Terror brought blessings in its train. The Christians were granted a second visitation of the Holy Ghost. The years following the Korean War show enormous activity in the Christian communities. The Young Nak Church received a constant influx of North Korean refugees. The Christian schools and universities, which had previously had only a few students, were now filled with thousands. The Presbyterian seminary alone enrolled 6000 students who wished to become ministers, which made it the largest Presbyterian seminary in the world. The Bible Club attained a membership of 70,000 all over the country. The churches built homes for widows and orphans. In the army, 350 posts for chaplains were created, with the result that today fifteen per cent of the South Korean Army is Christian, while the percentage of Christians in the population as a whole is only seven per cent. Seoul, which previously had thirty Christian congregations, now has 600. Pusan in the south, a city which had twelve Christian congregations, now has 200. Of the 150,000 North Korean prisoners of war, 20,000 were converted. Such things did not happen in any prison camps of the First or Second World Wars.

Thus the evil that the Devil thought to do was turned by God to blessing. The Lord heard his children's cry. In Psalm 34 we read, 'The poor man cried, and the Lord heard him, and saved him out of all his troubles.' And through the Prophet Jeremiah the Lord promised to come to the help of his people when they were in trouble among their enemies. It was given to the devout men and women of Korea to experience this blessing.

4. *A Curative Shock*

It was after the Korean War that I set foot on Korean soil for the first time. On arriving in Seoul, I got into contact with the Presbyterian church at the South Gate. I was invited to give a short address at the prayer meeting next morning. I was happy to agree, but a good deal surprised when I was told the time of the meeting — five a.m.

Five o'clock, and in that cold! The thought flashed through my mind, Who on earth would turn up? I went to my hotel. My alarm rang at four a.m.

Rain was beating against my window. My first thought was, 'The prayer meeting will be cancelled because of the rain.' I pulled the blanket up to my chin and tried to go to sleep again. I was unsuccessful. 'You must at least keep your word and put in an appearance, even if there's no one there but the minister,' I told myself. So at last I got dressed, rather reluctantly, and set off. It was not exactly encouraging to find that the taxi driver was asking double fare — still, I supposed he was entitled to the rate for night journeys.

The Presbyterian church came into view, a severe, very plain building with unglazed windows. Snow and rain blew into the church through the gaping frames. Yet again I told myself, 'You've come here for nothing. No one attends prayer meetings at five o'clock in the morning in cold, wet weather like this . . .'

I braced myself against the wind and entered the church. What did I see? My eyes nearly popped out of my head — the whole place was crammed with people. There were no seats; the congregation was squatting or kneeling on straw mats. I was staggered. I went up to the platform, quite at a loss, and turned to the leading brethren. 'What does this mean?' I asked. 'The whole congregation can't have been summoned to welcome one missionary!'

'This is our regular prayer meeting,' was the answer.

'What, in the middle of the week?' I asked incredulously. 'Not on Sundays when the members of the congregation have more time?'

'We come together daily,' they explained to me.

Again I felt my breath was taken away. 'How many people are there present?' I enquired.

'Almost 3000 — the whole congregation.'

I felt dazed, and asked no more questions.

One of the elders announced a hymn, and at once began to sing. There was no organ accompaniment, no hymn books; they had no musical instruments at all in this bleak building, which was more like a derelict factory than a church.

Then they prayed, all 3000 members of the congregation at once. If I had been told of such an occurrence before, I would have dismissed it as fanatical zeal. But I could feel the harmony of the Holy Spirit in this prayer. There was no disorder; it invited no comparison with the noisy praying of extremist sects. The people prayed for nearly an hour.

Then one of the elders asked me to give my address, adding, 'A short one, please, not longer than an hour. These people have to go to work at seven o'clock.' A short address lasting an hour! The words echoed in my mind. In what country of the Western world could the minister preach for an hour at a prayer meeting?

In any case, my sermon had quite gone out of my head while these people were praying. What had I to say to the

c

brethren and sisters present? It was they who had preached a sermon to me before I ever opened my mouth. In a spiritual situation of this kind I seemed to myself unutterably insignificant, tiny and pitiable.

This congregation needed no missionary from the Western world — unless it were for the missionaries themselves to learn the true meaning of prayer.

Next day, when I was talking to a missionary, I put these thoughts into words. 'What are we doing here?' I asked him. 'We are quite superfluous!'

He understood, and agreed with me. 'We are here to be shown what a community living in the spirit of the New Testament is really like.'

5. *Prayer Without Ceasing*

'Pray without ceasing!' the Apostle Paul wrote to the Thessalonians (I Thess. 5: 17). I have not seen this biblical admonition carried out so thoroughly anywhere as in Korea. Perhaps it may be the same today in the revivalist regions of Indonesia.

I had not yet recovered from the shock of that first prayer meeting before I found myself attending the next one. I was drawn into the wake of this throng of people praying. For the first time I really understood the words of Acts 2: 46: 'And they, continuing daily with one accord in the temple . . .' Daily! What have we come to in the Christian communities of the West? We pray for an awakening, and nothing happens — do we wonder at it?

At the third prayer meeting of the morning I asked the brethren, 'How often in the week does your group come together to pray?'

They replied, 'Every day.'

Three separate prayer groups meeting every morning!

'How long has this custom been in force?' I asked.

'Five years,' was the reply.

I began doing sums: 365×5×3 comes to 5474 hours of prayer, each attended by 3000 people. Should we not expect such prayer to reach the throne of God?

But I had not yet learnt everything; only in the course of a stay of several weeks did I gradually come to know all the wonderful secrets of this community of men and women of prayer.

There was a prayer service at night. Every evening a group of some 100 Christians met to pray. The groups alternated, of course, with different people coming together each evening — and every night for five years, a hundred members of this congregation had been in prayer until dawn. Once a week, from Saturday to Sunday, a thousand Christians prayed all night long. For the first time I was brought to understand the words of Acts 12: 5: 'Prayer was made without ceasing of the church unto God.'

Many other passages of Scripture took on a new significance for me. Leviticus 24:2 runs: 'Command the children of Israel, that they bring unto thee pure olive oil beaten for the light, to cause the lamps to burn continually.' The Roman Catholic Church, indeed, keeps a light constantly burning before the altar, but it is not so much a matter of having beautiful symbols in our churches as of keeping the hearts of the faithful burning continually, and never letting the flame, the incense of prayer, go out. The Korean men and women of prayer showed me the true meaning of Revelation 5: 8: 'Golden vials full of odours, which are the prayers of saints.'

6. *His Name Makes Strong*

After the descent of the Holy Ghost, Peter and John went to the temple. At the gate they met a lame man. The poor cripple expected the apostles to give him a gift of silver and gold. (Acts 3: 6.) Peter looked at him and said, 'Silver and gold have I none; but such as have, I give thee. In the name of Jesus Christ of Nazareth rise up and walk.' So saying, he took the cripple's hand and lifted him up. The lame man was healed at once and went into the temple with them, 'walking, and leaping, and praising God'. The onlookers were amazed by this miracle, and the apostles took this opportunity to spread the Word of God. Refusing to take any credit themselves, they proclaimed, 'And his name through faith in his name hath made this man strong, whom ye see and know: yea, the faith which is by him hath given him this perfect soundness in the presence of you all.' (Acts 3: 16.)

I would never have thought that I myself would one day be the witness of such an event. I had always been of the opinion that these miracles were privileges reserved for the early Christian communities. Naturally, I had never been a modernist and rationalist in my following of Jesus, but always believed, child-like, in the Word of God. But I had no factual material to illustrate my belief. I was to find it in Korea.

These congregations of men and women in prayer made no great ado about healing and the 'gift of tongues'. They hold a special prayer meeting for the sick only once a month. I was present at one of these meetings. I am quite unable to find words to describe my experiences on this occasion. All I can say is that here was none of the hysterical, urgent mode of prayer practised by extremist sects, but instead a revelation of the glory of God.

A lame man was brought to the meeting; several Koreans had taken turns to carry him eighty kilometres on their backs. Now the cripple lay there before the congregation. His weak leg and arm were shorter than the sound limbs. Prayers were said for him, and blood and the power of movement came back into the wasted limbs. The lame man stretched, stood up and tried out his healed limbs. They were no longer short; the sick, wasted leg and arm had grown to the normal length of the sound ones. The congregation did not make a great outcry as they prayed, but instead raised a wonderful hymn of praise to God. I would never have believed reports of this miracle if I had not seen it for myself.

Another sick man was lying on a stretcher, in the last stages of tuberculosis of the lungs. He was nothing but a skeleton. Blood blisters stood out on his lips at every breath he drew; he was a miserable sight. It was almost unbearable to look at him. The congregation prayed over him, calling on the name of the Lord. As they prayed, the sick man grew visibly better. He could soon expand his chest strongly; we saw him exercising his lungs and breathing deeply. He was completely cured by the hand of the Lord.

Words from the Bible again took on new significance for me at this prayer meeting for the sick. How often had I heard sermons preached on the text of St. Mark 2: 10: 'The Son of man hath power on earth'! I had often been fortified, too, by the words of II Chronicles 20: 6: 'In thine hand is there not power and might?' But I have never seen such proof of the power of His hand as I did here, among these men and women of prayer.

A boy came into the midst of the congregation and asked them to intercede for him. His hand was withered, so that he could not move his fingers. He confessed his sins, putting his life into the hands of Jesus, and then the congregation prayed over him. As they did so, blood surged into his withered hand. We could see the boy's joy when he found that he could use it; he grasped objects standing near and played with the healthy fingers, an expression of indescribable delight on his face. What a Lord is this, who can work such miracles in the twentieth century! And what a judgment on the lukewarm Christianity of the West that we have reached the point where we can no longer believe! I was in that state myself; I would have doubted all this if I had not been an eyewitness.

On these occasions I was constantly repenting of my own sins; I was almost crushed to feel the Lord so close. For there is a considerable difference between reading of such miracles in the New Testament and being permitted to witness them oneself. Language is inadequate to express the holiness and glory of the presence of the Lord in any fitting way.

After my return from Korea I told a Western congregation of my experiences, and a minister asked me, 'Will you pray with the sick members of my congregation, and heal them in the name of the Lord?'

I replied, 'How many people have you in your congregation?'

'Two thousand,' he answered.

'How many of them attend your prayer meetings?'

'Twenty or thirty of them meet once a week.'

I told him, 'I am ready to pray with your sick — on condition all two thousand members of the congregation meet to pray at five a.m. every morning for five years.' For that was what they did in Korea. We are giving ourselves unnecessary pains as long as the conditions of the New Testament do not prevail in our own communities.

The outstanding feature of these prayer meetings for the sick was the peaceful manner in which they were conducted, with none of the usual whipping up of spiritual fervour. When extremist groups offer us 'healing', what do we find? If their claims are investigated either they turn out to be false, or the cures are only psychosomatic and temporary.

7. In the Spirit of the New Testament

Before I attended this prayer meeting for the sick, it had been in my mind to tell the congregation assembled there that a man's salvation is more important than his cure. I intended to say to them, 'Preach the Word! Forgiveness of sins is greater than healing of the body.' I did not carry out my intention. What we in the West present as good theology, applying to biblical times, is actually carried out in practice today by these simple, devout people.

As I have already mentioned, out of thirty prayer meetings there was only one for the sick, the rest being devoted to the worship of God and intercessions of every kind.

Another characteristic of Korean Christians is their readiness to make sacrifices. They give financial support to the preaching of the Word of God in a way I have never met anywhere else in the world.

Many of these devout people are rice farmers. In spite of the biblical rule that the labourer shall be the first to enjoy the fruits of his toil, Korean Christians do not take advantage of the latitude allowed them; they sell their rice and buy millet, which is half the price. They give their profits — that is to say, fifty per cent of their earnings — in aid of missionary work, to send missionaries to neighbouring countries and so spread the Gospel. They give not a tenth, but a half of all they earn.

This example should be an eternal reproach before the throne of God to the satiated Christians of the West. In what superfluous plenty do we seem to live when we consider such sacrifices!

Moreover, in the face of such faith and devotion, can we still wonder that all the miracles of the New Testament were manifested again in the Korean revival? I admit that I had always doubted whether the dead could be raised in the twentieth century. Since my first visit to Korea, which was later followed by others, I have doubted no longer.

In these devout communities, men physically dead have been restored to life, but more, many more, of the spiritually dead returned to life. It put me in mind of the words of Jesus, 'I am the life.' How easily we use this as a pious saying! And when it really is a matter of belief, we bolster up our unbelief with theological arguments!

Along with the shattering events experienced by these men and women of prayer goes the observation that the message of the Cross is central to life and to the preaching of the Gospel. This is why my original plan to tell these people something of the meaning of the Cross appeared to me pitiable, if not positively ludicrous. These Christians were actually living out what I intended to say.

The Korean revival has nothing to do with the Pentecostal movement of our times, nor has it anything in common with faith-healing missions, or with other charismatic movements of the present.

Korean Christians conduct themselves temperately; their revival is one of biblical clarity, with no ecstatic manifestations on the periphery. The Lord Jesus is glorified. The Holy Ghost is at work, but no attempt is made to constrain Him or subordinate Him to our wishes, pious as they may be. This is the Pentecostal atmosphere of the Acts of the Apostles.

The centre of the revival movement of 1907 was Pyongyang in North Korea. The central point of the second wave of the revival was Seoul in South Korea. The

Spirit of God blows where it listeth, not where we plan and wish it to blow.

And now, what is the present situation of the Christian Church under the Communists in North Korea? We have already touched upon this subject; let us return to it.

8. *The Underground Church*

Recently there has been much controversy in Christian publications about the existence of an underground Church. For instance, a man who had spent four weeks in Rumania wrote to say that Pastor Wurmbrand had given a distorted impression of the situation there. It is strange, admittedly, that someone who has spent four weeks visiting a country can claim to know it better than a man who has lived for fifty years in that same country.

To ensure that I had reliable witnesses, I got into contact with three devout Rumanian ministers and asked them whether Wurmbrand's account of the situation was correct or not? All three confirmed the truth of Wurmbrand's assertions. One of these three Rumanians had himself spent seven years in Communist prisons, and had suffered tortures similar to those inflicted on Wurmbrand. The second said that the church to whose congregation he ministered had been confiscated by the Communists, and since then the people had met to pray out of doors, many kilometres away. The third, who is still in Rumania, wrote and told me that he was not allowed to spend more than two days away from his community without informing the authorities in advance. In addition, he is not permitted to preach to any congregation but his own, and he may address his own only within the strictest limits.

Why should the truth be thus distorted by tourists paying brief visits to a country? Well, the facts are well enough known; it is not always done with malicious intent. How, then, do such reports come into being?

I can illustrate this point by reference to a Russian example which, with some modifications, applies to all Communist-controlled countries.

Moscow has a theological seminary. Yes, that is correct — there is a centre of theological education in the Red capital! 'There!' say our tourists who visit the place for four weeks. 'If the state is educating priests, you can see they have religious freedom in Russia!' But what is the real purpose behind this seminary? Let us trace it. A devout young Russian, who had been converted to Christianity, proved to be so fervent a follower of the Lord Jesus that he wished to become a priest. In good faith, he applied to the theological seminary in Moscow for training. He received a discouraging reply from the authorities, informing him that only those picked by the government might study there. However, this devout man, J. S. from the village of M., was pertinacious. He was not to be put off so easily. So he was unceremoniously arrested and condemned to three years' hard labour. It is difficult to grasp such a contradiction in terms. The tourists certainly do not understand it; they are conditioned, by means of soft words and good entertainment, to return to their own lands with rose-coloured accounts. But anyone who is acquainted with the system knows the game the Communists are playing.

This theological seminary in Moscow is run by atheists. Some young Communists are deputed to study theology there; they then become priests, the official pastors of the Russian Church, in order to spread atheist and Communist doctrines veiled in theological terms. The most tragic aspect of the whole business is that they derive many of the tools of their trade from modern theology. Western theologians are forging weapons with which the East can persecute Christians. It is easy to understand all this — incredible, however, that Christian tourists from the West will publish garbled accounts of the situation in Western newspapers.

The distortion of information from the East is one of the most diabolical aspects of contemporary life. I will add the story of a revealing incident that I had at first hand. Two prominent ministers of Western congregations (not of the Established Church) were visiting Rumania and met the Rumanian Minister of Culture. One of their first questions was, 'For what offence has W. been imprisoned?' Of course the arch-Communist replied, 'For political offences', and in so saying he was correct! In the eyes of the regime, the conversion of Communist functionaries by the testimony of a Christian *is* a political offence. We can hardly brand the Minister of Culture a liar for saying so. The really shocking thing, however, is that these two Western churchmen reported the Communist politican's pronouncement to their congregations in the West as the last word on the subject. Yet more shocking is the fact that there are papers which will publish such distortions of the truth to the Christian world as a piece of news.

The story of the 100,000 Bibles is another tragic example. My source of information is a devout Rumanian who, like Pastor Wurmbrand, was imprisoned for many years and often tortured for the sake of his faith. He told me the story of the printing of Bibles in Rumania. Before the Communists came to power, the British and Foreign Bible Society had been sending Rumanian Bibles into the country. Thank God for this Society. For many years after the Communists seized power, the parcels of Bibles were turned away, though a number did get through. Recently an arrangement was made between the Rumanian government and the Bible Society, whereby the government allowed the printing of 100,000 Rumanian Bibles, while the Bible Society, for its part, was to stop sending copies. They promptly delivered the paper and all that was needed for the printing of the 100,000 Bibles to Bucharest, and the Communists promised to get them printed. The Western world breathed a sigh of relief, seeing this as a relaxation of the Communist system, and Christian newspapers happily announced the printing of 100,000 Bibles in a Communist country, taking it to be a symptom of religious freedom. What are the real facts behind this action? In many districts of Rumania, lists were drawn up; anyone who wanted a Bible could put his name down. It was a thoroughly successful manoeuvre. The Rumanian secret service now possesses the names and addresses of all these readers of the Bible. Now let us look at the other side of the coin — where *are* the 100,000 Bibles? No bookshop has them on display. No one knows where to obtain them. The Rumanian government has managed, quite legally, to stop deliveries of Bibles from abroad. Communism has won this move — why do we not see through tactics like these? Of course, after the publication of this pamphlet, which is first appearing in a German edition of 30,000, a few Bibles may be displayed in the Bucharest bookshops, just to show tourists 'what lies they tell in Western countries'. And yet again tourists on brief visits will be taken in, and contribute further to the duping of the gullible West. Such blindness is a punishment, the judgment of God upon us, and it will only be recognised as such if world Communism should ever succeed in taking the Western world unawares, which God forbid!

One argument frequently expressed by those who set out to dupe us is the claim that there *is* no underground Church. What are the facts of the matter? Anyone looking for an organised underground Church, complete with bishop and consistory, will not, of course, find one. No such thing existed in the catacombs of Rome, and other cities of the Roman Empire. When Paul went to Syracuse he held his services not in the temple of a Roman god, but in the conduits of the city, which are still to be seen today. The Christians in Communist countries risk arrest to meet in private houses, cellars, barns, hiding places in caves and woods. They are not organised from outside, but the Lord Jesus is in their midst. If two Soviet soldiers are converted and meet in secret to pray, they do not belong to the official, Communist-controlled Church, but to the underground Church, a true community of Jesus. An underground Church is inevitable so long as godless men, atheists, and those who deny Christ control the official Church. As the first edition of this pamphlet was going to press, news came from Hungary that a declared atheist had become Minister for Religious Affairs. In all Communist countries such measures inevitably lead to the formation of small, illegal cells of devout Christians.

So much for the basic situation. I will now return to the underground Church in North Korea. Who are my informants? I was the guest of a number of North Korean refugees. My most reliable source of information is Dr. Han, of Seoul, who worked for many years in Pyongyang in North Korea. He is a friend of Billy Graham, and the best-known minister in Korea. He was chairman of the World Congress for Evangelisation in 1968 in Singapore. On November 24th, 1968, in Seoul, he gave an account of the situation in East Asia. His secretary gave me a copy of it. It is a magnificent speech on the theme of closed and open doors (Revelation 3: 8, 20).

Dr. Han said:

There are doors opened wide to the Gospel in South Korea, Japan, the Philippines, Indonesia, Taiwan, Hong Kong, Singapore, Australia and New Zealand. On the other hand, other countries are closed to the

Gospel, among them North Korea, Red China, and Burma. In these lands the Communists have bolted the doors. Buddhism places obstacles in the way of the Christian mission in Nepal; a Nepalese who is converted to Christianity and baptised goes to prison. In Afghanistan it is Islam that closes the doors. Conversion to Christianity incurs the death penalty. In Malaya and in Singapore, the Chinese form forty per cent of the population, and are free to choose their religion, but the Malay population may belong only to Islam. India and Ceylon guarantee religious freedom, yet Christianity is not fully accepted in public. In Pakistan, Islam puts many hindrances in the way of the Gospel.

This is the view of a man who has travelled in most of these countries. What is the situation in North Korea?

Reprisals were made against North Korean Christians even during the Korean war. After the end of the campaign Christians were forbidden to hold any religious services. A dummy organisation, the so-called 'Christian Alliance', was founded to provide documentary proof of religious freedom for the benefit of other countries. Its chairman, Dr. Kang Nam Ook, is a pawn of the Communists. The official Church is committed to the Communist government, just as it is in Russia and other Communist countries. Was not the World Council of Churches in Uppsala the best proof of this? Most of the bishops from the East were puppets of their Communist governments.

But there is a secret Church in North Korea too, one that has not bent the knee before Baal. Let us look at it.

Polling took place in 1957 to elect the people's assembly in North Korea. The officials counting the votes in the city of Yongchun were surprised to find that several thousand of those entitled to vote had not done so. This upset the city fathers, since it meant that they could not send in their full quota of votes. There were Christians in Yongchun, but it could not be proved that the missing votes were theirs. However, it had been noticed that the turnout of voters was usually very small on a Sunday, and the authorities based their suspicions on this. The secret police went into action. Christians were sought out in their houses. They were at home on a Sunday, but not available for interview. The police made further enquiries, and at last hunted down the missing men and women in secluded places where they had met for prayer.

Many Christians were interrogated after this discovery. It came out that Yongchun alone had some 500 such prayer cells, so that every Sunday the underground Church had several thousand members of its congregation meeting secretly. Naturally the secret police were interested in finding the organiser of all these cells. One of the men responsible was Mr. Lee, a former minister from another district, now working on a collective farm. In his free time he did personal missionary work, and formed those Christians he had converted into the cells I have already mentioned. Lee and several other prominent Christians were arrested and condemned to death.

Another account comes from the city of Pakchun. A Christian woman teacher taught languages, mathematics and music, and in her music lessons she taught the children Christian hymns as well as the prescribed Communist songs. The children sang their Christian songs with enthusiasm at home. Of course this could not remain a secret for long. In the new wave of arrests the teacher was imprisoned, and so were those parents who had not forbidden their children to sing hymns.

Yet another event deserves our attention. One day an old man appeared in the city of Sun Chun. He was called Father Kim. He had obviously lost his reason, and would wander around the streets talking to himself, often glancing at the sky and making a gesture of his hand towards the south. This brought him to the notice of the police, who made enquiries about his past and discovered that he had been a Catholic priest. They therefore arrested him, and he was condemned to be shot. Just before his execution he prayed out loud, in a clear voice, 'Father, forgive them, for they know not what they do.' Then he was shot. If the two halves of Korea should ever be re-united we shall hear of many other martyrs whose stories are as yet unknown.

The story of another incident comes from Wonsan. A workman dropped a small cross he had been wearing round his neck in the shower room of a factory. He was denounced and arrested at once, and forced to tell the secret police where he got his little cross. As a result the Communist executioners discovered many Catholic Christians living in Wonsan and the surrounding area, and the leaders were called to account.

Such incidents prove that the doors are closed in North Korea. However, there is a living underground Church, consisting of Christians who meet in secret places to pray and fortify themselves with the word of God to continue their struggle. There is not much we can do for our brethren and sisters who live in such danger. We can only pray for them and send them messages of comfort by radio through the Iron Curtain.

9. The Clouds Gather Again

Twelve years passed between my first and second visits to Korea. In the meantime, the accursed Vietnam war, so closely resembling the Korean War, broke out. The Communist North is intent upon subduing South Vietnam, and never allows its opponents a breathing-space. The

Americans are fighting for the South, as they did in Korea. But the situation is rather different. During the Korean War, thousands of Christians were on their knees every morning. This is not the case in South Vietnam, though there are small, devout Christian communities there too.

South Korea follows the course of the Vietnam war with the greatest interest, since its outcome will have repercussions on Korea. The South Koreans were thunderstruck when the President of the United States let it be known that he would not stand for re-election, but would do all he could to end the Vietnam war. I happened to be at the Evangelical Academy in Seoul when this news appeared in the press. Dr. Kang, the Principal of the Academy, was horrified to hear of it. He told me, 'At the East Asian Conference of Churches in Bangkok I used all my influence to show my colleagues the dangers of abandoning South Vietnam. The Russians represent the Americans as interventionists, yet it was the Russians who crossed the demarcation line from North Korea and attacked the south, not the Americans who attacked the north. In Vietnam it was again the Communists, the Vietcong, who attacked South Vietnam, and not the Americans who attacked them. If the Americans leave South Vietnam to its fate, not only will the whole of Vietnam become Communist — all the other free lands of East Asia will follow suit in the course of the next ten years. A peace treaty in Vietnam means war for all those lands of East Asia that are not yet Communist; above all, it means appalling terrorism directed against the Christian Church. With a Vietnam peace treaty forced into being by world opinion, the pacifists of the West will give peace to the Communists, and war, oppression and slavery to everyone else. It is nothing short of a disaster to see a large part of the American people stabbing their government in the back.'

D

Dr. Kang is not the only Korean to think along these lines; he expresses the feelings of a thousand others.

After the election of Nixon and the partial withdrawal of American troops from South Vietnam that was negotiated at the Paris peace talks, the alarm of the South Koreans increased.

When I was giving a lecture at a large college with some 1200 students, I got into conversation with the Rector. He told me, 'We just can't understand the Americans' naivety. President John F. Kennedy was assassinated by the Moscow-trained Communist Oswald, his brother Robert was shot by Sirhan Sirhan, who wrote in his notebook, "Communism is the best social system", Dr. Martin Luther King was killed by Ray, a tool of world Communism — and yet the Americans cannot see what is going on!'

Then this Christian teacher added his personal creed. 'In the dreadful disorder of the past few years, we Korean Christians found our only refuge in prayer. Our problems were not solved by political and military action alone, but by prayer, and so it will be in the future too. We will go on praying.'

To go on praying — that is no tranquilliser for the weaker vessels. We Christians have no other weapon but prayer. We know that God will not abandon His post; He is no old man losing his grip. His long silence is not a sign of weakness, but a proof of patience. Nor have the problems of a world ripe for judgment grown too much for Him. He will bring His people to safety, even though they pass through the catacombs, and at the end of all suffering we shall see the fulfilment of the words of Psalm 29:11: 'The Lord will bless his people with peace.'

Chapter III

THE YOUNG NAK CHURCH

After the lapse of time between my first and second visits to Korea, I was interested to find out whether the flame of the revival was still burning, or whether it was near extinction. For it is a mysterious and baffling fact that the tide of spiritual awakenings always seems to ebb after a few years or decades. The revival in Wales did not even last a decade, although of course its effects were felt much longer. What amount of strength and stamina did the Korean revival display?

Let us examine this question in the light of the community life of the Young Nak Church, the most prominent among hundreds of communities.

1. *Tradition or Life*

My story is set in Seoul. It was the fourth Sunday in Lent, called *Laetare* — 'Rejoice ye!' And it was a day that began joyfully; the reading for the day concerned the figure of Abraham. 'He staggered not at the promise of God through unbelief; but was strong in faith, giving glory to God; And being fully persuaded that, what he had promised, he was able also to perform.' It was an inspiring passage from Romans 4.

The next stage of this Sunday seemed unlikely to be very joyful. I wanted to leave the C.V.J.M. Hotel at half past four in the morning to attend Dr. Han's prayer meeting. I was on the seventh floor, and the lift was not

working yet, so I walked downstairs. There was an iron door between the sixth and fifth floors, and it was closed. Back I went to my room! I telephoned reception. No answer for a long time. Finally there was a sleepy voice.

'Will you be kind enough to open the door for me?' I asked. 'I want to go to the Young Nak Church.'

A cross mutter was all the reply I got. I went back to the lift. Not a sign of life. Back to my room again! A second telephone call, and then a third. At last something happened; the porter, roused from sleep, let me out by the back door and immediately shut it again behind me. I was out in the hotel yard.

Act Two — all the doors from the yard to the world outside were closed, and the night watchman was nowhere to be found. It felt like being in a prison yard, surrounded by high walls. I was reminded of the time the Russians had put me behind such walls.

Then I saw a light in the cellar. Down I went to the basement. There were enormous boilers there, radiating heat, and a boiler-man sitting by them. I spoke to him in English, which he did not understand, while I could not understand his Korean. I showed him my Bible, indicating with gestures that I wanted to get out of the building. He pointed to the night watchman's lodge. I made more gestures to explain that the night watchman was not there. At last he understood, and went off to look for the man who had the key. We finally found him.

During this complicated manoeuvre I was thinking, 'What would happen here in case of fire? No one could get out!' In fact, as I learnt later, twenty-nine people had burned to death a year earlier in a large building locked like this one. However, it had taken me half an hour to get out of the C.V.J.M. Hotel, and I should not reach the prayer meeting in time on foot. I hailed a taxi. When I got

out the driver cheated me; his meter was not working (they usually don't work when Asiatics are driving foreigners).

I arrived, ten minutes late. A prayer meeting held from five to six a.m. — how many times a month? By now you will be becoming familiar with Korean habits of prayer. These meetings are held, not once a month, not even once a week, but every morning! There can hardly be any communities in the Western world where such things occur. Is that a fact? Well, I do know one minister who meets some workmen in his church every morning at six a.m. for a brief service of morning prayer. It lasts ten minutes. I have not come upon hour-long prayer meetings held every morning in any Western congregation.

A hundred people had met to pray in the Young Nak Church, or rather in an adjoining room. Dr. Han himself was taking the service. At the end of it he introduced me to his congregation. As we went out I was thinking that I could do with some breakfast after all the exertions of my attempt to get out of the hotel. And I got my breakfast. What did it consist of? Dr. Han took me to another chapel, near the main church, where I saw the second prayer group, which met from six to seven a.m. How often did this group meet? Again, every morning!

You might be thinking that this fatigued me. Not so; I knew no Korean, but I could feel the spiritual atmosphere around me, and I could pray in my own time.

The minister then explained the various Sunday services to me. 'The first public service takes place at seven a.m.,' he told me. 'Since you have had no breakfast, please leave the second prayer meeting before the end and come to my house.' So at six-thirty my stomach got some food inside it.

Half an hour later I was sitting in the church at the first early service. The building holds 2200 people, and it was

already full at seven o'clock. The second service was at ten a.m. Yet again I was astonished by this remarkable community. The church was full once more! The third and main service was at eleven thirty, and as for the attendance, there was not a seat empty. This is the service that foreigners attend, because the sermon is translated into English over a monitoring system.

Children's services are held at the same time as the main services, attended by about 2000 children and young people, grouped according to age.

In the evening the congregation assembled for the sixth time. Adding together all the services, including those for children, on a single Sunday, the attendance figures for this one community were about 12,000. No other community in the world can point to such figures.

What is the secret of this church? The congregation is not assailed by rhetoric, but the power of the Holy Ghost brings them into the presence of God. These are the fruits of the Korean revival.

Billy Graham preached the Gospel here some years ago. At the World Congress for Evangelisation in Berlin he made the following comments: 'Anyone who has not yet come to know the Young Nak Church and has never heard it pray does not know what a prayer meeting really is.'

Surely this revival in Korea, which has now lasted over sixty years, is a great gift of God! It has not yet cooled off into a dead, mechanical empty form of tradition. There is still life and vigour in it.

I have never before had such an interpretation of *Laetare* Sunday. Rejoice ye!

2. Dr. Kyung Chik Han

Dr. Han is one of the most prominent spiritual leaders of
Korea. Before I give a brief account of his life, I must add
a note of warning. Biographies usually set out to glorify
human beings. Of such books it may be said that they are
robbing God of what is his. Honour to whom honour is
due! Whether we are concerned with Billy Graham in
America, Peter Oktavian in Indonesia, Dr. Han in
Korea — who are they? Mere sinners who have been
taken up and chosen by the Lord. Great as a man's life
work may be, every man of God, every evangelist and
missionary, is exposed to the dangers of egotism, and all
the more so when God has entrusted great things to
him.

Once we understand that we must see everything in its
relationship to Jesus, we can describe our human subject
as the tool of God.

It seems to me that Dr. Han's life falls into two distinct
parts: his career up to the founding of the Young Nak
Church in 1945, and his work of reconstruction in South
Korea after the founding of this community.

The Choice and Preparation of the Tool

Dr. Han was born several kilometres north of Pyongyang
in North Korea. As I have already said, this city marks the
extremes of the spiritual history of Korea. It was the
source of the great revival in 1906; today it is the anti-
Christian centre, the seat of a regime that persecutes
Christians savagely. One Christian church has been left
open there, to demonstrate religious tolerance to those few
tourists who obtain a visa for North Korea. In this way the
Devil has succeeded in getting a footing in the Holy

Ghost's own camp. But his triumph will be short-lived. The time is coming when God will make an end of the beast from the abyss that tyrannises over Asia today. He to whom God the Father in Heaven has entrusted all power will make the last move in the game.

Thus Dr. Han comes from the part of Korea most under stress. At the beginning of this century, the slight, wiry boy could not know that he himself had been chosen by God to play a decisive part in his country's history. He was only five years old at the time of the revival; the movement had no direct effect on him, but indirectly he got a great deal from it, as we shall hear.

At first he was a cheerful boy, usually the leader of his contemporaries because of his merry yet determined nature. His cheerfulness was not at all impaired when, a little later, he heard of Christianity and the revival from his older cousin, a Confucian scholar who had turned to serve the Nazarene. After this good man was converted he was so inspired by the Gospel that he preached it to all his dependants and relatives. It was through this former follower of Confucius that a Christian community was formed in Dr. Han's native village.

The converted Confucian, feeling a strong urge to lead many people to Jesus, started a Sunday School. Han was among the pupils. An American missionary, Dr. Blair, who was still alive at the time of writing of this pamphlet, used to visit the school twice a year. The young Han, with his bright, lively eyes, attracted Dr. Blair's attention, and a friendship which has now lasted over fifty years sprang up between them. Dr. Blair watched over his young friend's career, and advised him on all questions of his education. It was on his recommendation that Han attended the Academy at Chung Joo. Later he entered the Presbyterian Union Christian College in Pyongyang. At

the same time as he took his four-year training there he was acting as secretary to Dr. Blair, who had taken him into his house.

It was at this time that young Han had an experience which decisively influenced his future development. While he was walking by the shore of the Yellow Sea, the Lord stood in his path. He threw himself down and stayed there in prayer for some hours, giving himself up wholly to Jesus. As he did so, it became clear to him that he must take up the work of the Kingdom of Heaven.

Dr. Blair arranged for him to follow a course of study in the United States. At first Han attended Emporia College. Just before his examinations he had an attack of influenza which kept him in bed for two weeks. However, he passed his examinations, and his results were among the highest. He continued his studies at the Princeton Theological Seminary, from 1926–29. Here too he graduated with the highest honours. He earned money for his studies by working as a dishwasher in hotels and bars.

Soon after finishing his studies he fell ill with tuberculosis of the lungs, which crippled him for two years. Because of his weak constitution there was not much prospect of a cure. Han had to come to terms with the idea of death. It was a hard path for a hopeful young man to tread. He submitted himself to the will of God, but after intensive prayer he knew the joy of conviction that God would cure him, as indeed He did.

Once he was better, he was appointed Professor of Biblical Studies at the Soon Sil College in his native land. But the Japanese put obstacles in the way of his taking up this appointment, so instead he contented himself with a ministry in Shinui Chu. His work in this community laid the foundations of his future pastoral labours, for which he has become known not only in Korea, but all over the Christian world. He realises today that this is why he was

barred from taking up his academic post by the Japanese — the experience of working among his congregation was to fit him better for his future duties. The end of the Second World War marks the end of the first stage in the life of Dr. Han.

3. *Reconstruction in South Korea*

Dr. Han's work in Seoul began after his flight from North Korea, where the Communists had made it impossible for ministers to continue their work. Moreover, Han's patriotic spirit could not bear to see the subjugation of his people, and the spiritual outrages inflicted on them.

It was hard to start again in the south. Like the other refugees, Dr. Han did not know at first where to live, where to work, or what to live on. He met several North Koreans who had been as completely uprooted as himself, and suggested that they might meet for prayer. There were twenty or thirty of them. After their prayer meeting they felt so comforted that they decided to repeat it. These meetings of despairing men were the first seed of the community that was to come into being. By the spring of 1946 this community, which had given itself the name of the Young Nak Church, had 500 members. By the summer of 1947 the number of members had risen to 2000. They then had to begin holding several services every Sunday, because of lack of space. In the summer of 1948 there were 3000 members of the community to be cared for.

But these gatherings of North Korean Christians were not the end of the story. The refugees' children needed to receive a Christian education. They therefore founded the Tae Kwang Academy, which today has 1500 pupils. Dr. Han (who was given honorary degrees by an American university and by the University of Seoul) is chairman of the board of this academy.

Over the years, the congregation of the Young Nak Church grew to such an extent that it became necessary for them to build a church of their own. Plans were drawn up in 1948, and building began at once, the members of the community contributing their own voluntary labour. They all helped actively in the work, from grandfathers to grandsons. The church was built with much prayer, and by the work of the hands of its own congregation. It was a fine building with 2200 seats, dominating that whole area of the city from a hilltop, like a Gothic cathedral. Three weeks after it was dedicated, the Communists attacked and Seoul had to be evacuated.

It is impossible to gauge what this new flight meant to the North Koreans. They had already lost everything once, and were they now to be delivered to the Reds again? In addition, they were distressed about their recently finished church.

At first Dr. Han stayed on in Seoul. Several elders of the church kept him in hiding. When the Communists marched in and began systematic house-to-house searches, his friends urged him to flee. He agreed, and set off for Taegu, a journey of some weeks on foot.

Then the U.N. troops and the Americans recaptured the fallen area, and even liberated Pyongyang in North Korea. Han was close behind the troops, and so he was able to conduct the thanksgiving service for the liberation. The North Korean Christians had many tales of suffering to tell. Only those who had been able to go into hiding were still alive; the others had been slaughtered by the Reds. North Korea alone has thousands of martyrs. Yet the bishops and dignitaries at the World Council of Churches in Uppsala acted as if they knew nothing of such things, and accepted the overtures of peace made by their Communist-backed colleagues from the East. To adhere strictly to the truth, it must of course be admitted

that there are a few high dignitaries of the Eastern Church who are *not* shepherds by the grace of Communism.

Dr. Han's thanksgiving service in the liberated city of Pyongyang was premature. The Chinese sent in large contingents of soldiers, who advanced rapidly, and by Christmas had reached Seoul again. For the third time the North Koreans fled.

A day before Christmas the church's orphans were sent south. It is to the everlasting credit of the Americans that their air force flew a thousand children safely to the island of Chejudo. Dr. Han, with 500 members of his congregation who had stayed behind, celebrated the Christmas service. It was the most emotionally tense service he had taken in his life.

After the service Dr. Han was summoned to see President Syngman Rhee. He was asked to read out in public the government's decree that the city was to be re-evacuated, a task that shows what Dr. Han's position was in the public eye, and in what esteem he was held by the government and the people. Although the Communists had ravaged Seoul, the Young Nak Church had suffered only a few hits and was otherwise unharmed. For the thousands of faithful members of its congregation, this was an answer to their prayers. The church could be repaired quickly.

I need not go into the whole history of the Korean War again. Dr. Han was asked to go to Japan and take up a ministry there. He declined, with the words, 'In these times of trouble, I cannot leave my people and my congregation here.'

God had need of this man in Korea, and it is hard to measure the full extent to which God blessed him and used him as His tool. His work and prayers brought many good things into being. An orphanage, a widows' home, a

Bible Club, a high school, and the academy I have already mentioned were all financed. Training was provided for twenty-three evangelists and missionaries, and their stipends were guaranteed. The Synod of the Church of Korea chose Dr. Han as its moderator. He also sits on the board of many official bodies, a task which often leads to the spiritual death of a great man . . . has Dr. Han gone over to the side of the religious activists?

No — Dr. Han not only does sit on the boards of all these organisations; more important, he is present at his congregation's five a.m. prayer meeting, and has been *every morning* for twenty-five years. I was able to see the truth of this for myself, and his secretary confirms it.

In this life it often happens that the men with most responsibility fall victim, spiritually speaking, to the activity of their lives. In spite of their religious calling they become ambitious, a burden to those around them, and victims of complacency — and never notice it. It is those in close contact with them who feel it and suffer for it. In what light does the Young Nak Church regard its minister?

I heard many of his qualities mentioned to me. It is said, to Dr. Han's credit, that he regulates everything he does by prayer. When he is talking to someone he will always say, 'First let us pray.' This is the secret of the authority that can be felt when he stands in his pulpit on Sundays. One would hardly think that so strong a voice could come from so weak a body. However, it is not the power of his voice that moves men, but the Spirit of God hovering over this congregation.

Others praise Dr. Han as a man who has never been seen in anger. In fact, some people have tried to provoke him on purpose to test him. They did not succeed. Dr. Han remained imperturbably friendly to his tempters.

He is also famous for his mature, impartial powers of

judgment, and is said to be extremely quick to grasp and explain difficult problems.

Not last, an important point — Dr. Han is the opposite of avaricious. As his secretary told me, 'That man does not know what he earns. His wife always collects his stipend and looks after him devotedly, which is necessary, for he gives away everything he has in his pockets. If he meets a beggar he will put his hand in his pocket and bring out all his money, and then go long distances home on foot because he has nothing left for a fare.'

If I were asked what most impressed me about the Young Nak Church, I should say:

1. The way in which the Holy Ghost is present in this congregation.

2. Dr. Han, that quiet, humble man of prayer, who never thinks of himself, a priestly soul who comes before the throne of God every morning with his congregation.

Here is a man in whom Christ has manifested Himself. We should honour and give heed to this man as a spiritual father and leader of Korea, and we should give even more honour to Him who glorified Himself through this man: the Lord Jesus Himself.

Korea is not yet finished; the Christians of Korea are at their posts and praying. So long as Moses kept his arms raised in prayer, in the battle against the Amalekites, (Exodus 17), the children of Israel were victorious. So long as Korea's Christians continue to pray, the Communists will not prevail, even if they should conquer South Korea too. Military force, and terrorism backed up by party politics, cannot suppress the Church of Jesus. The final victory belongs to the Crucified One, and the army of those who pray to Him.

Correspondence may be sent to the author care of

THE CHRISTIAN MISSION TO THE
COMMUNIST WORLD,
P.O. BOX 19,
CHISLEHURST,
KENT,
BR7 5AA.